Indeed You Can

A True Story Edged in Humor to Inspire All Ages to Rush Forward with Arms Outstretched and Embrace Life

Elleta Nolte

CCB Publishing
British Columbia, Canada

Indeed You Can:
A True Story Edged in Humor to Inspire All Ages to
Rush Forward with Arms Outstretched and Embrace Life

Copyright ©2011 by Elleta Nolte
ISBN-13 978-1-926918-53-2
First Edition

Library and Archives Canada Cataloguing in Publication
Nolte, Elleta, 1919-
Indeed you can : a true story edged in humor to inspire all ages to
rush forward with arms outstretched and embrace life
/ written by Elleta Nolte.
ISBN 978-1-926918-53-2
Also available in electronic format.
1. Nolte, Elleta. 2. Texas Tech University--Students-- Biography.
3. Adult college students--Texas--Lubbock-- Biography. I. Title.
LD5314.N65 2011   378.764'847   C2011-902658-9

Cover artwork by: Micah Nolte

Publisher: CCB Publishing
            British Columbia, Canada
            www.ccbpublishing.com

To my longtime friends
Jeanetta, Reed, and Eloise
Their years equal 268
But their strength and spunk
equal youth in its prime

Also by Elleta Nolte

Westward, Ha!

For the Reason we Climb Mountains

Gray County Heritage (co-editor)

Little Chapel of Brookhollow

Chapel of Brookhollow (revised and updated)

A Place Set Apart

Deeds & Misdeeds of an Indian Territory Doctor

At eighteen, I knew little except at thirty I would know everything

At thirty, I knew I knew little

At forty, I was too busy to know if I knew anything

At fifty, I knew the more I knew, I would never know enough

At sixty, I was grateful to know the little I knew

At seventy, I knew how to know; I enrolled in college

At eighty, I toted textbooks, finished finals, graduated at 89

At ninety, I flirted with graduate school, found tuition too steep

At a century of my age coming up, still I am learning

*T*hese words "still I am learning," translated from Italian "Ancora Imparo," and credited to Michelangelo, are inscribed on a necklace given to me. The words symbolize my inherent nature. God gave me two indisputable traits for learning: curiosity and motivation, along with the distinct drive to turn defeat into determination, to turn "No, I cannot" into "Indeed, I can." But I was long into life before I realized these qualities, for I was painfully shy and inhibited in my early years. I believed anything I could do, anyone else could do better, an ingrained streak that sometimes hovers and keeps me humble. My mother dragged me to a little country school three mornings before she could disentangle me from her side and enroll me in first grade.

Perhaps my timidity and fear of people outside of my immediate environment was due in part to the fact I was a child of the Great Depression and its most disparaging forms of poverty, as were many others in Oklahoma where we lived. When my parents divorced in my early teens, my mother and I had little means of survival. In order to remain in high school my senior year, we rented an apartment for $3.00 a week, while my mother kept house for a large farm family, working seven days a week for $3.50. (Looking back, we wondered what we did with the extra 50 cents a week.)

But in the midst of deprivation throughout these years, something unexplainable within me promised, "In time I'll learn and achieve much." The vow remained, for shortly after high school graduation in 1937, I dated a young petroleum engineer who proposed marriage. Although I cared for him, I turned down his proposal with the assertion, "I have things to achieve before I marry, and no, we cannot do them together."

Those "things" began when my mother and I

moved to a small town in New Mexico where we lived in a one-room shack for three months. This enabled me to attend a business training school during the day and to work as a carhop at a drive-in during the evening. The training led to another place and position in late 1939, to the small town of Pampa in the Panhandle of Texas and the early-day Radio Station KPDN.

Radio work and I became well suited, but I changed locations, for my curiosity and motivation surfaced as I realized the tremendous changes occurring in our country, and I had seen little of other places. Not long after the attack on our naval base Pearl Harbor, Hawaii in December 1941, I rode a bus across the map to Seattle, where my brother lived. In answer to my resumes to radio stations, three job offers awaited me. I accepted a position at KIRO, the most powerful radio station in the Northwest during the war years, with its transmitter on Vashon Island. The personnel found my accent unique, and they always addressed me as "Texas."

I was enchanted with Seattle, the beautiful city built on hills, its parks strewn with rhododendrons in brilliant colors, with ferries to enticing islands in

3

Puget Sound, and with Saturday night USO dances for the many servicemen who awaited further orders. Their images remain in my memory: John, a soft-spoken sailor from Alabama; Garth, a self-seeking airman from Maine assigned to Officers Training School; and Ray from Michigan, the one I could have fallen for but did not. The one who had a fiancé back home.

I left Seattle and KIRO in October 1942, and returned to Texas to Pampa, now dotted with servicemen, for the city had lured an Army Air Force base to establish nearby. It was there I met Quenton, a newly recruited tech sergeant from Iowa, one of the first five enlisted men to activate the field (and the last to leave the base after its closure). Shy, dark-haired, and handsome, I thought he could have doubled for movie idol Tyrone Power. My shyness briefly took a holiday, for shortly after we met, I dropped a telephone number and a comment to his co-worker, "If Quenton doesn't ask me for a date, I'll ask him." Quenton called that night and showed up at my door. It was Halloween, and he always said I tricked him. I did. We married in January 1944 in the little chapel at the Air Force base, followed by an eventful 63 years that blessed us with nine children. During that time, I found that indeed, I could do a great many things.

As my single years were seldom dull, neither were the long years Quenton and I shared as we worked to provide for our growing family. Yet even now, it's difficult to realize the major step we took in 1960, the action culminated in my book, *Westward, Ha*! Its flyleaf gives a glimpse of the struggles:

When the Noltes and their eight youngsters left a comfortable and secure life in Texas to establish an uncertain homestead on a section of intractable sagebrush in a remote part of Nevada, they had no premonition of the real price one can pay for an independent venture. Their trials run from the animosity of a quick-tempered rancher who had long leased the land for cattle, to a hasty retreat from a major flood that drove them from their home—this in the driest state in the union. In spite of the obstacles of dust, heat, wind, water and errant cattle that threatened that first important crop on new land, the

Noltes gained a patent for 320 acres of land. They later sold the land and returned to Pampa in Texas in 1962.

We established our former ties with Pampa, and settled into life in its usual course of happenings. Quenton opened a bookkeeping and tax office; I accepted an office job at Cabot Corporation; the children finished their education, moved onto their chosen careers, and created their own nesting. Life became secure and satisfying.

But it was not to last. Our fourth son, Alan, graduated from Texas Tech University in Lubbock and Baylor School of Dentistry in Dallas and began his dental practice at Cleburne, Texas. On a spring day in 1978, he died while scuba diving, leaving a wife and two small sons.

After Alan died, I became deeply depressed, sensing emptiness, sadness and withdrawal; emotions of that depth were strange and unusual for me. I continued to sink in despondency, though I never confided in anyone.

Perhaps this period of depression had a bearing on the life-changing event that occurred in 1985.

One day I simply opened my mouth and without any thought beforehand, blurted out a question to Quenton: "If I find a house near a lake would you move?" He answered, "Yes." Little discussion followed; it was simply something we felt we were to do. In a domino effect of events within a few months, we sold our home and Quenton's business and bought a house overlooking a lovely lake in a small West Texas town with the intriguing name of Ransom Canyon. A section from my book, *A Place Set Apart,* describes the site:

For miles and forever miles, the flat and featureless land with its sweeping beauty of space and freedom spreads out in all directions from Lubbock on a high dry plateau on the South Plains of Texas. Suddenly and dramatically, the flatland falls off the edge to a full depth of 190 feet in a deep, wide canyon on the Caprock, a canyon that grew a town in the 1960s.

At age 66, we began a new chapter of contentment and fulfillment in our lives. The Texas area, home of the Comanche Indians for 150 years, lay ripe for research and its telling, while my curious nature caught the uniqueness of Ransom Canyon, and I began fact-finding and writing. Quenton became involved in civic activities and served as mayor for a term.

But *enough:* this writing is not about all those earlier years, it's about what additional things I discovered I could do with my curiosity and motivation in advancing years. Age was only an illusionary figure in my life, not to be taken seriously. I found I could enroll at a prestigious university as a freshman at age 71 after 53 years from high school graduation. My college graduation at 89 inspired many people of all ages to say to me, "You need to tell people what you did, and what they can do, that age can have a positive effect on their lives."

This is that telling.

*A*lthough I thrive on goals, I never listed enrolling in college as one to reach. If it had occurred to me, my logic would have dismissed the thought and moved along to more attainable targets. Six of our nine children graduated from Texas Tech University in Lubbock, so I knew of the entrance tests required for institutions of higher learning, and clearly it was not for me.

But maybe it was. I believe God gives us each a path if we open our mind and heart to accept it. He knows our unique nature, and plans our paths accordingly, giving us the graces we need to complete our goal in life. God doesn't deal in limitations; our perceived limitations mean nothing to him. We must work with them, through them, or around them.

So perhaps this was his plan for me, for conveniently in the fall of 1990, Texas Tech dangled a tantalizing carrot in front of would-be older students. In a program called Senior Academy, Tech offered streamlined admissions and registration procedures for students 55 or over. The university required no transcripts or SAT/ACT scores, but once admitted, a student maintained the same academic standards, and paid the same tuition and fees as traditional students. I was among the first to inquire, take a tour of the campus and enroll. I would handle my self-imposed limitations.

Two of my college-seasoned daughters, Marsha and Tricia, took my hand and led me to register for classes and obtain my ID, textbooks, and parking permit. Bewildered kids followed parents all over the campus that enrollment day. This bewildered parent followed kids.

Later we did a dry run: "Mom, park here and wait for the bus. Get off here. Walk to this building. Go in this door. Here's your classroom and the restroom. Here's your next class. Go out this door and wait here for the return bus."

More words to the unwise: "Sit on the front row. Record the lectures. Enter into class discussions. Talk to your professor during office hours if you need help." I wondered if the girls would check my homework and report card.

We shopped for new jeans, shirts, and sneakers. I said I needed a book satchel. "No, Mom, you need a backpack—here try this one. No, not on your back, slip one arm through this strap." (The rest dangles and flops.) I decided privately I would sneak out and choose my own lunch box and crayons.

Later, as I sat reading a textbook in preparation for my first class, my daughter Tricia called me. I complained, "College is too hard. I've read three pages in a book, and I don't know what they say. I may drop out." She gave an enormous sigh. I hoped I would not become a problem child. They had such high hopes for me.

At that moment, a profound surge of emotions—an epiphany—set me back in my seat. I had come full circle in my life. When the time

11

came for my children to begin a new and exciting phase of learning in their young lives, I took the hand of each of the nine and led them, observed and encouraged them, through all the years of schooling and into successful careers. They, in turn, now closed the circle, extending the same love and care to their mother in her new venture. Perhaps the master planner held my hand also, to lead me in a new direction on my path. Now I waited to see what came of this new impulse of mine born of the desire for personal growth and achievement. I smiled in contentment, picked up my textbook and continued reading.

As I drove away from home for my first 8 a.m. class, I glanced at the sunrise's billboard in my rearview mirror. It seemed to ask, "Where you going...the beauty and things you love are back here...why are you leaving?" And it nagged, "The flower beds need clearing, the bird baths need cleaning, and..." I waved nonchalantly, "later...the other kids are calling me."

The campus swarmed with the other kids as I struggled to find the classroom for my first English class. A bit late, I stumbled into the room and stared at the sea of faces. One student asked, "Are you the instructor?" I answered, "No, I'm a freshman," and I sat down. Later, I climbed to the third floor of the building, and as I stood looking out across the vast campus dotted with students, the immensity of the turn in my life hit me, and I felt a great surge of excitement at the prospect of what might lie ahead. I thought, "This is my school, this is my building, I am a college student, I am so privileged." And I turned away in tears.

I didn't stay in my first English class after the third day, however. I sought out my English advisor and Director of General Studies and explained to him I didn't believe I could learn in that course, "It teaches you to write, and I know how to write," and I showed him two of the books I had written. He looked at my writing, then handed me a list of classes and said, "Pick out the one you want." I glanced at him and suspected he thought, "…what the heck, she's not going to last anyway."

As it turned out, my advisor had another thought. Tech sent me a copy of a letter he sent to the Associate Dean of Arts and Sciences. In it, he requested I be allowed to substitute two advanced

English courses for the two required freshman composition courses. "I have examined a book and several articles Mrs. Nolte has published," he wrote. "As a result of her own self-education, she has attained a level of writing ability far beyond the capabilities of most college graduates. It would be an immense waste of her time and talent to take the freshman courses, for she is far beyond what they cover." He suggested the advance courses would "enable her to write critical essays more challenging to her writing ability."

I, the lowly freshman, the one with the inflated head who could select any advanced English course, chose a junior class of short stories, taught by the head of the English department. I found the classroom, walked in and then stood uncertainly as I glanced around at the small class. The professor asked, "Can I help you?" I explained I was enrolled in his class, and he answered, "You can't be, my class is full...but, oh well, sit down."

I sat on the front row and listened with rapt attention to the discussion of the short stories. Yet later when the professor handed out the first test, I was so traumatized I could scarcely read the questions, even though I knew many of the answers. I flunked the test, completely bottomed out. And I thought, "wait till my advisor learns of this." Devastated, I swallowed my pride, crawled into my instructor's office and asked for help. With his suggestions, I earned a B grade in the course with upperclassmen. As an ironic note: it took this writer a fourth of the semester to learn to write a critical essay in the preferred form.

It didn't take long to learn I fit on campus, however. Anyone I regularly saw over fifty was either personnel or professor, yet I never felt my age as a student was a factor. I was just another individual, another body. The other kids started a conversation with me as I did them. I strode across campus and caught the bus back to the parking area, as did they. The bus was often packed, and I stood and swung from the strap, but oddly enough, I gained a measure of satisfaction in that the students did not offer me a seat; we were fellow students, and I didn't expect nor want any special treatment.

I greeted each day on campus as a new beginning—the best of the rest of my life. I felt forty of my years melt away when I set foot amid the rushing, bustling aura of the campus filled with the leaders of tomorrow. I seemed to absorb their vibes as they scurried along, ponytails bobbing in rhythm with sandaled feet, caps set at individual angles. In a refreshing way, I felt akin to their youth, their vigor, their dogged determination to keep working and learning to attain their goals, however uncertain those goals might be at that stage of their lives. I wasn't a finished product; in my heart I was young again, anxious to test new ground and gain new knowledge.

I had lived so long I gained a certain layer of insulation. The things that tore me apart in my lifetime had taught me to let things work out, to hand them over to God and follow his will. Now in this new chapter of personal growth in my life, nearing its finale, I wondered what I might yet achieve.

This desire for achievement was leading me in strange yet gratifying directions, ones that my offbeat sense of humor welcomed. Perhaps my many years surrounded by children conditioned me for my place on campus, surrounded by swarms of students. I could so easily laugh at their occasional comments, *"But why…why would you want to do this…what are you going to do with a degree?"*

And in a light moment, one student asked, *"What are you going to be when you grow up?"*

As I exchanged quips with another student, he asked, *"Just how old are you anyway?"* I laughed and told him and then added, *"I know what you students think; you look at me and ask yourself, 'whoa…is it gonna take me that long to finish?'"*

Later I had a comment from the professor in my electronic media class, "Introduction to Telecom-munications." He wrote, *"I never knew I would have a student older than radio."*

Now that is old!

I learned I even outlived my high school. The College of Arts and Sciences informed me they needed a copy of my transcript of 1937 in order to process my degree plan. I explained it would be difficult, if not impossible to obtain a transcript since I had graduated 56 years ago, and the small school no longer existed.

Even though I am quite average in intelligence —and grateful for that much—I probe and push my mind out of low gear into second, and on good days, shift it to high to reach its limit, and it never occurred to me but that I could learn as easily as the other students. I passed the then state-mandated TASP test after nine hours, tested out of two English classes, and moved on to other basics and classes toward a General Studies Degree, designed to provide the foundation of a liberal education through a well-rounded study of the humanities, arts, math, behavioral and natural sciences. I chose to concentrate on the extended studies of History, English and Behavioral Sciences.

I related my classes to the Ropes Course I saw at the Tech Recreation Center described as: "High elements provide opportunities for encouraging others, taking risks and accomplishing tasks that at first seem scary and even impossible."

Accomplishing tasks...this I do. I set my own bar, my own aim, my own risk-taking. Something indefinable led me from the first course, to the next course, to the last course, not from any deep seated desire to "get a college degree," but to start and finally finish, for this is what I do—I finish what I start. Michelangelo expressed it quite reasonably: "The greater danger for most of us lies not in setting our aim too high and falling short, but in setting our aim too low and achieving our mark."

As I walked on campus, I often stopped and sat on one special bench at the corner of the Chemistry Building and Memorial Circle. It bears our son's name, a memorial to him given to us by our children. The plaque reads:

Alan R. Nolte, 1950-1978,
BS Chemistry TTU 1972, DDS Baylor, 1976

He filled his lifetime with humor, love, and compassion and met challenge with unwavering grace. He's at peace with God. Rest and let Alan's spirit inspire you to work with passion, achieve your dreams, and live in love.

In January 1992, another heartbreaking tragedy struck our family when our beautiful and talented 16-year-old granddaughter Courtney died. She and I were very close; she was proud that her grandmother was a college student, and she always reminded me to keep up my grades.

After I accumulated 34 college hours and stepped over the first bar to become a sophomore, I took a hiatus of six years from Texas Tech to celebrate our golden wedding anniversary, finish a book I was writing, prepare our house for sale in Ransom Canyon, and build another in Lubbock.

But the lure of learning called me back in 1999, and I reentered Texas Tech to finish my degree. In deference to my age of 80, I enrolled in Extended Studies, classes via mail, fax, email and online. Tech initiated a provision whereby a student 55 years or older is waived up to six hours of tuition per semester. Clearly a bonus! Later, Tech abolished this option for Extended Studies students, but they left mine in place as I "grandfathered" in. The provision remains in place for on-campus courses.

I found help and encouragement for students in many areas of the campus, from the open-door policy of the instructors, to Mandy Corcorran, senior representative in the Office of Extended Studies. She became my sideline cheerleader; she scheduled my courses, encouraged me, and pelted me with compliments and smile-giving words, "You're an outstanding student and you rock most high, Sweetie." Mandy read an article written about me by the *Senior Gazette,* a news type publication in Lubbock. She emailed me:

You have no idea how many people you influence. I have your picture in a frame with your story hanging on the wall in my office. A co-worker read it, and it inspired her to go to real estate school. She completed her courses and is now working part-time with us and selling houses the other half of the day. She said your story proves you are never too old to go back to school.

My age was of little concern to me——I was too busy studying. However, some things I sought to learn and did not. My love of reading may have evolved from my parents; neither received any formal education although they became avid readers. But in time I learned I could not read and absorb the beauty and power of poetry. Some intense, rambling verses left me empty. But I tried. I enrolled in "North American Poets," a little excited about at last finding the key to appreciating poetry. Our professor explained in the syllabus that some students could not grasp poetry. My first clue. Seated daily in a large circle to discuss Walt Whitman and his "Leaves of Grass," she instructed us to read aloud several passages and give our reflections. I read the passages all right, but then I sat in silence. I had no reflections. I was grateful for the privilege of dropping classes.

But I have a passion for history; my classes ranged from "History of Civilization," to "Religion in America," to a fun course, "History of Baseball," among others. In an independent study course, "Reading and Research in History," I gained three hours credit for a history book I was writing. Other favorite courses were four psychology courses and a superb course in Cultural Anthropology regarding Indian heritage.

In "History of the English Language," I chanced across a word in the *Old Oxford English Dictionary* that identifies me precisely. I am an opsimath. The Greek in 1656, adopted the word opsimathy that means "learning attained late in life." The word was used as a put down with implications of laziness and considered less effective than early learning. Two centuries later, in 1883, the *Chicago Times* stated, "Those who gave the name were not simple enough to think that even an opsimath was not something better than a contented dunce."

Ah... but this dunce was doing well, for my GPA remained a B-plus, though it fell somewhat after two required courses in Spinach...uh, Spanish (I read that spinach was difficult to digest, as was Spanish for me). My kind, gentle professor wrote to me, "Let me confess that I think you are one of a kind...to have the stamina to engage yourself into coping with Spanish."

I had the stamina, all right; I gave Spanish more coping time than all the other courses, but it remained very complex for me. Later, I read that learning a new language is a struggle for older students, depending on whom you asked. One 57-year-old student interviewed on the Internet found Spanish hard to learn. No one asked an 88-year-old.

My family, always supportive, was in a surprise party mood when I finished Spanish. I stepped into a room swarming with family and friends wearing colorful tee shirts inscribed accordingly: *Mi esposa / mamasita / abuelita / suegra / amigo / yo paso la clase de Espanol a la Universidad de Texas Tech.* Translation: My spouse / mother / grandmother / mother-in-law / friend / passed the Spanish class at the Texas Tech University. It was my first time to laugh at anything Spanish.

Except for Spanish tests (when I prayed a lot), I never saddled myself with worry or stress during the courses. In typical student style, I walked into the test center thinking I had studied as much as I could. I walked out thinking I should have studied more. But all things concerned, I did well, though my grades did not match those of my granddaughter Rebecca who also attended Texas Tech. Separated in age by a stretch of 64 years, she was set to graduate with me.

*T*hen in spring of 2007, as we planned our 20th annual family reunion, my whole world crumbled. My husband, recovering from medical conditions, suddenly worsened and died on March 20. It was one of the most intense days of an emotional upheaval in my life, for I love deeply, and I grieve deeply. Quenton was my rock, my protector, my helpmate, my inspiration. We shared a love for 63 years. He encouraged me from the first to finish my degree, and now, almost at once, everything changed.

Besides the grief at my loss, the prospect of living alone, and facing the deadline of a science course in which I was enrolled, I received a bolt from Social Security. It listed Quenton's death as occurring in 2006, rather than 2007, and sent me a statement to recover a year of benefits. Four days later, the Treasury Department emptied my checking account without contacting my bank or me, letting my checks and drafts dangle.

As distressing as all this, I began to take stock of my life and to soothe my troubled mind. Could I bring it to focus again on classes? Or would I spend the time in suspension, erasing this one goal I set for myself? I was scheduled to graduate the next spring, the date set firmly in my mind. The decision whether or not to continue was eminent as the deadline to finish my science course lay just ahead. I took my dilemma to Mandy in the Tech office, and they extended the deadline another month.

After I completed the science course, I looked hesitantly ahead to finishing the last four courses to graduate, one fine arts course and three math courses (one a remedial course with no credit). I knew math would be a struggle, for the only thing I remembered was fractions in the fifth grade, yet I registered for the first math course. Previously I would have dived into the remaining courses and finished them, but now I left the math course un-touched. My mind still struggled with all the weigh-ty issues of grieving, plus my banking dilemma still existed. Now a new challenge arose: I began to have nightly hallucinations; it would be some time before they would subside.

Suddenly math and my long-term plans no longer mattered. I began to think of the most im-portant things in my life, and maybe being smart was to know when to quit. Leaving college had never entered my mind, but now in an almost au-tomatic response, I emailed Tech to withdraw from the university. Tech responded immediately ask-ing me not to withdraw, and offered me two courses of economics as a replacement for math.

Grateful for Tech's interest and concern, min-gled with what was left of my motivation to finish what I started, I emailed my answer and registered for economics.

Then a record of sorts occurred: two of my granddaughters, Alisha, a Tech graduate, and Me-lissa, nearly so, tutored me in the economics courses after they first visited my instructor in his office and asked how they could help their grandmother with lessons. Later, he emailed me, "You have wonderful granddaughters. They are not the only ones impressed by your desire to learn. You're doing what only few even think of doing. We are all very proud of you!" I earned a B grade in the two courses and moved on to my last *Hallelujah*, the lovely fine arts course, "Heritage of Music."

At last, this opsimath, this contented dunce, was set to graduate from Texas Tech University on May 10, 2008. The planning committee informed Rebecca and me that we would march and sit together during commencement. But they felt the graduates' long winding entrance march into the rotunda of the arena might prove difficult for me, so as a first step, they seated us in the huge space to wait and join the other graduates when they appeared.

Rebecca and I sat in the hushed atmosphere within the eyesight of a thousand or so spectators with the only scene in front of them—empty seats and us. I had the absurd notion of how enlightening it would be if we rose and moved in slow fairy-like motions, our long black gowns swirling, to the center of the vast space, where we would pause, pivot, remove our caps, and then bow deeply in each direction and to each other. Would anyone applaud...would anyone dare?

Rebecca and I joined the other kids and we marched to the solemn strains of "Pomp and Circumstance," to be seated for commencement. We passed the long line of faculty members who stood motionless as we appeared. Their faces wore a bit of boredom and perhaps fatigue as they stood the second day for the fifth ceremony for over three thousand graduates. But their eyes widened, and disbelief flashed across their faces as they saw me, an older worn model of graduates. I could only smile.

We graduates sat together, composed and quiet, listening to the speeches. When we were told to flip our tassels—we were graduates—I felt a great gush of accomplishment as if I could jump up, kick my heels together, give a whooping yell and shout, *"Yes!"* I had achieved something difficult, started it and finished it. I interacted with people different from myself who had an impact on my life. I challenged myself over some compelling odds. I graduated from college.

I also felt a tremendous desire to put my arms around that huge chunk of kids and hug them, for who they were, and what they had achieved, the many I knew who held one or more jobs to help pay for their education, and those who struggled with other issues.

The speeches over, we stood and marched in line to receive our diplomas. The line suddenly stopped when my name was called, and I received mine after a bit of explanation about me to the crowd who spontaneously applauded. Rebecca, next in line, graduated magna cum laude with a degree in English.

Afterwards, Tech placed us together on a bench nearby while the other graduates filed out. We became a little giddy at this point and whispered back and forth, leaning closely to hear each other, the black and red tassels on our caps aflutter.

I thought of the many steps I had taken, one by one, that led to this day, steps for the sheer pleasure of learning and the joy of fulfillment. I could have spent the days in trivialities, in actions of little importance or value; instead I exchanged those actions for these productive days of my life. I could also have withdrawn earlier in the face of defeat, but my path did not lead in that direction. Somehow in there I gained a measure of self-respect as I gave a small inward salute to the scared little girl in first grade.

In the afternoon, our family staged a huge backyard bash, a fun, hallelujah, no-more-finals party for the two of us. Leigh Ann, my youngest daughter, found a shirt in a fitting fashion for me. (Note the hole in the back of my head in the picture on the next page.) Granddaughter Christi, with a Masters Degree from Texas A&M, explained to me: "The hole comes with your degree, your brain slowly drains after you receive your diploma."

From the beginning, I wanted to graduate with one of my grandchildren, for I wondered if my attending college was in part for them, as their love and admiration poured out to me in words and shows of affection that overwhelmed me, in grand gestures that made all the work worthwhile.

Rebecca's letter touched my heart:

Experts say how important it is for parents to read to their children to instill in them a love for reading. I have a picture of you as you sat reading a book to my brothers and me, and when I look at that picture I think about how you've gone above and beyond that. You still continue to set an example for everyone in the family to keep on reading, to keep on writing and to keep on learning. I'm lucky to have been given a wonderful grandmother who still encourages me in words and examples to always keep going no matter what I do, so thank you for that.

Eight of my other grandchildren graduated before me, including Jason, Alan's son, who finished at the University of Texas. He wrote: "You were an inspiration to me to go to school, graduate and pick up the pieces of my life. I don't know I would have done that had you not started your degree."

Michelle also graduated from the University of Texas. She wrote:

I hope you're getting a degree for yourself and not to meet our expectations. It encompasses how truly amazing you are, always challenging yourself, stepping out of the ordinary, following your own path. Your passion for research, learning and writing makes us proud because you never let go of what you love...your face lights up.

Micah and Alisha, who finished at Texas Tech, and Jeremiah, my ex-Marine grandson, congratulated me, "It gives the rest of us something to strive for."

And in a way, I shared my graduation with Courtney, forever sixteen. Her last words to me were: "Keep up your grades, Grandmother." I did that, Courtney.

I left Texas Tech with a rich store of knowledge and memories and experiences, ones I continue to savor. A great deal of knowledge passed through the connected pathways of my brain, far more than I could analyze at once, and a bit of it lodged there, waiting to be recalled. A friend of mine said, "I couldn't retain all that knowledge." I laughed, *"Retain?* Nobody told me I had to retain it; all they said was I had to register for the courses and pass the finals."

Yet even before the finals faded, I knew I was not quite ready to rest on my laurels. I was still in a learning mode. The smidgeon of learning I acquired was only that—a smidgeon. It whet my appetite for more. The one thing left undone in my mind's eye was to gain a Masters of Science in Human Development and Family Studies with emphasis on Gerontology—the science of aging (I've had experience in that). It sounded relatively simple, 36 hours, online courses, no GRE required. I inquired and it was so tempting—and the tuition so costly. Besides, when I mentioned this to my family, they got real quiet, and I thought I saw the color drain from their faces.

It was only after I graduated I realized how much I learned about myself, who I am and what I am and what I can do. I thought back to the students' earlier questions: *"But why...why would you want to do this...what are you going do with a degree?"*

And I thought of another small episode that occurred later. I met three Tech seniors who heard I had just graduated, and in deeply concerned voices, they asked, *"Do you have a job? Have you sent out resumes? What kind of job are you looking for?*

I smiled at the realization that I was, after all, what I wanted to be—one of the kids on campus. The answers to their questions lay within myself.

Age does not change us. We become more of who and what we've always been. Age simply piles years upon us, but our basic instincts remain the same. I've always been productive, creative, and busy—oh, yes—always busy, and I remain the same. As with many of us, I spent most of my life doing what was required of me, what lay in front of me to do. Now, subconsciously, I had simply reached a time in my life when I wanted to find *me,* to see what I could achieve, what I might become. When that part of my path opened and opportunity beckoned, I rushed forward, arms outstretched and embraced it.

As I finished my courses, I began to feel my years of work were indeed part of my path and had another purpose. At graduation, a few reporters and television crews hovered around, and briefly I added to the news of the day, an 89-year-old great-grandmother who graduated from college with her granddaughter. Then I began to hear from other people and in particular, younger ones who had dropped out of school and not gone back, they who were "too tired, too busy or too old" to start again and finish their degrees. Many of them found me to say, "I needed to know that; you need to tell others what you did, that it's never too late to learn."

Recently, two of my daughters and I spent a weekend at a Benedictine Monastery nestled in the Sangre de Cristo mountains of New Mexico. While there, a woman approached me and said, "I understand you graduated from college at 89; I came here this weekend to ask God if I should go back to school. I'm 57. I just want you to know I have my answer."

Maybe in a very small way, I made a difference. Mandy, my college representative said, "You have no idea how many people you affect." Maybe she was right; a teacher in Amarillo, Texas, wrote to me, "You are having a great impact on my GED students. I have the picture of you and your granddaughter taken when you graduated. When my students get discouraged, I just bring out the picture. It is an instant "pick-me-up.""

Of course, as with anything worthwhile, my learning took its share of time. Of even more importance, I lived another full life alongside the demanding one of being a college student. I gave quality time to my roles of wife, mother of nine, grandmother of twenty and great-grandmother of ten.

I gave quality time also to writing regional history, and during my time at Tech, I wrote three books: *A Place Set Apart*, the history of Ransom Canyon, Texas where I lived, and the history of the *Chapel of Brookhollow,* and later its revision and update. These, as with my previous books, involved in-depth interviews and endless research in libraries, museums and county clerk offices as far away as Illinois where I researched for my latest book, *Deeds and Misdeeds of an Indian Territory Doctor.* I also edited a monthly newsletter and made six oral presentations to the West Texas Historical Association.

During this time, Quenton and I continued to travel (my textbooks often went along); we went to Europe three times, once on a religious pilgrimage, another an anniversary gift from our children, and again for the sheer joy of going. We also toured Canada and the New England states and other places to add to our visual memories. Oh, and another travel trip: we soared with the birds in separate hot air balloons over a portion of West Texas for an anniversary gift.

Over achiever? No. We are each given the same amount of time in a day and a choice of how to use it. We set our own bar. My curiosity and motivation always kick in, for I believe to *be* something more, we must *do* something more. Many of us subconsciously retard our own intellectual growth. We reach the stage of our own personal point in learning and place our mind on idle for the rest of our time. We place our bar too low and limit our possibilities. I simply choose to keep learning.

You out there: if you have a desire for more education and choose college, you'll gain self-confidence, knowledge and skills you'll use for the rest of your life. It will increase your understanding of the world and its people and will broaden your understanding of other cultures as you meet students from varied backgrounds. You'll learn abstract theories and concepts you might not learn otherwise. College will give you practical benefits as well: graduates have a wider array of job opportunities and a chance to earn more with a degree.

No career in mind? Many students do not decide at once, sometimes only when they finish their basics and even then, they sometimes change their major. If you choose a school of higher learning, you'll be exposed to a variety of academics and new perspectives. Occupational tests exist to help you decide.

College too difficult? Only if you think so. It's vastly different from high school. It requires more discipline, organization, and studying, but it's well worth the effort. Indeed you can handle it, if you believe you can. And help is out there, for the universities offer tutoring and student support. If you meet with your instructors and ask for help; you'll receive it promptly.

Can't afford college? It's expensive, but most students receive financial aid based on need, so the less money you have, the more aid you might receive. On a personal note: I told our children they could become what they wished if they were willing to work for it. Six of them earned university degrees; the other three received degrees or certificates in other chosen areas. They all have excellent careers today. All nine earned their own education, including some master degrees and a doctorate, with scholarships, grants and loans, while working summers and during school.

School takes too much time? Oh, come on now, I won't touch that—the lamest of lame excuses.

Think you're too old? Think again. In fact, as age increases, so can confidence and capacity for concentration. Young students have no real advantage to learning, for older ones often think with more depth and reflection. They have a wealth of experience and insight the younger students lack, so they can relate a new concept to a fact they already know, hence they can better grasp that knowledge. They've lived through a legion of history and political phenomena and have amassed a world of knowledge along the way. A bit of memory sharpness loss may occur over time, but years of experience make up the difference.

Research reveals advanced age does not lead to universal or inevitable cognitive decline. The decline is speed of learning, not intellectual power. The response time may be reduced, but not significantly. It may take a little longer to solve complex problems or remember facts, figures and names (the lost word at the tip of the tongue happens to all ages), but the power to think is the same as with those younger. Many never lose the potential to learn new things or master new skills. It's not age that determines mental skills, but motivation and the amount of stimulation a person receives. Any mental functioning that may decline over the years can be reversed once a person begins to study and learn again.

Learning at the college level for all ages is becoming more convenient, for universities clear across the country offer courses entirely at a distance, with access to student service representative only a phone call or mouse click away. The beauty of it is that you take the classes at your own pace, at your own place, and you may enroll at any time. It's possible to register, submit assignments via mail, email or fax, meet your deadlines, find an approved proctor, and receive your diploma, but never step foot on the campus. I gained the larger portion of my degree through Texas Tech University Division of Outreach and Distance Education at Lubbock, Texas.

In regard to tuition, a number of states have public college tuition waiver programs. Some offer discounts. If textbooks and tests are not for you, however, adult learning centers exist that require neither. Or perhaps you might want to simply audit courses, and reduced rates apply to these as well.

Consider also the two-year public community colleges that are excellent choices for many people. They offer affordable education with training and lifestyle learning courses in a variety of areas, whether you're considering an associate degree, an occupational credential, or plan to finish your studies at a four-year college.

If you're more technical minded, you'd find that technical training has evolved enormously over the past few decades. Once known simply as "vocational classes," designed for students not college-bound, some of today's courses are classified as "Career and Technical Education." These courses include analytical skills as well as technical skills and are more aligned to industry needs.

We hear: "Not everyone is college material." True, it isn't the goal of all students, nor should it be. Many feel they are not suited for academic study, yet to reach their potential, they may need an inner push to gain career training in some other area. One of my sons, offered help in funding for college, turned it down, remarking, "I can't see spending that much time and money for something I don't need." I left his statement alone and waited. He created his own path, and today he has an excellent position in the Bureau of Diplomatic Security in the U.S. State Department, working in American embassies across the world, a position that fits his unique skills and talents.

An option for lifelong learning that includes travel is Road Scholar. It's the new name for the programs of Elderhostel, the nonprofit travel and educational organization that staged guided tours in the U. S. and abroad for 34 years for seniors 60 or older. It changed its name to Road Scholar in 1975 and opened enrollment to adults 21 or older with shorter and more flexible itineraries. They offer programs in all 50 states and more than 90 counties. The website: www.roadscholar.org

You may think your success in the goal you set depends in great part on outside influences and other people. Not always true. Place your goal upfront in your mind, and let your positive thoughts push you along to reach it, for to a large degree you are what you think. Henry Ford knew this well: "Whether you think you can or think you can't, you're right." The Book of Proverbs in the Bible teaches, "As a man thinketh in his heart, so is he," while the famous psychologist, William James said, "A person can change the circumstances of his life by changing his thoughts and his attitudes."

The point is, if you desire change in your life, only you can make it happen. If you're looking for a new direction, a path to follow to affect the rest of your life, then plant that first step down your path. What have you always (or lately) wanted to do or become—a teacher, fireman, hairdresser, electrician, policeman, pilot, dentist or work in the medical field? Set your sights on what you wish for yourself. Put a little daring in your life, add a few "what ifs" and follow through, what if I...

A universal consensus seems to exist that as we age, our mind enters into a gray area in which the fog only thickens. In a large part, we have allowed that to happen; oldness and its collection of terms—old codger, fogy, gaffer, geezer, old lady, biddy, squaw, and more, and its old jokes (some quite good) have floated around for possibly forever, and in a way, give us a chance to laugh at ourselves.

Television often beams us seniors as doddering and disarrayed and barely able to function, our minds outdated and outworn. The media views our aging as the light-casting beam of a headlight: At 70 we start to flicker, at 80 to fade, at 90 to flash feebly, and at 100...well, that model is on the way out.

Hold on there...not so fast...the old jokes about the aging process are wearing thin. We are living longer and thriving today. The elderly are the fastest growing segment of the modern population. Thanks to better diets and medical care, we're healthier, which means our energy level is rising, reversing the downtrend age gives us. Many of us are becoming "indeed we can" people: we recharge our batteries, ignite our zest for life, plunge into new interests, open our intellect to learning, and set new goals. And in the process, the negative images of ageism grafted into our minds are fading, particularly in recent decades as increasingly seniors in their 70s through 90s are accomplishing some inspiring achievements.

Even hearty, sturdy centenarians amaze, inspire and delight us. Oklahoma's oldest resident is 110, according to *Tulsa World* in December 2010. Ora Holland of Tulsa lives alone and manages some household chores. Up until about two years ago, she was push-mowing her lawn and still driving a Buick Century (she was issued a speeding ticket when she was 99). Besides being independent, she's described as "alert and very astute," although she can't recall the name of her second husband. "We were only married for about three months," she said.

Many oldsters have learned the answers to aging is within themselves; they have given their past to God and look only forward, finding that tomorrow is full of promises. My spunky little friend from third grade, Jeanetta Love, is just shy of a century, but she has little loss of memory, hearing, seeing or mobility, driving herself to church and to shop or visit friends. She lives near a little town in Oklahoma on wooded acreage she mowed and trimmed until recently when her son discreetly disabled her mower and "forgets to fix it."

Another superb example of aging with grace and gusto was my cousin, Mamie Price, slender, petite, and gentle. She lived her 104 years in the small town of Vega in the Texas Panhandle. She kept an active mind with reading, crossword puzzles, and seeking to solve puzzles before the contestants on the game shows. Mamie was a champion domino player, maybe because she used her mind, "I pay attention, and I don't talk all the time," she said. "The rest of them talk and they have to be told when to play."

Mamie always said, 'I'm never going to get old; I may age, but I don't have to get old." She did things other people felt they were too old to do; in her 80s she sometimes jumped on the trampoline with her great-grandchildren and got in the swimming pool with them.

I went to Mamie's 103rd annual birthday party held in the Oldham County barn at Vega, filled with 300 guests. Mamie knew each one, never forgetting a name. At the last of the party, her son-in-law glanced at the band standing by ready to play, offered his arm to her and said, "Mamie, let's dance." And dance they did.

Mamie outlived three of her seven children. She never did get old. She just added years onto a beautiful lady. In 2008, at the age of 104, Mamie gently went to sleep. In all probability, she awakened to the enthralling strains of a choir of angels.

Will I live to be 100? Maybe. Check back in eight years.

Another unique lady has received worldwide recognition for her keep-learning philosophy. Nora Ochs of Kansas City, Missouri, only two years shy of a century, never seems to get old, and she has the credentials to prove it. Ochs, 98, received a Master's Degree in Liberal Studies in May 2010 from Fort Hays State University. She earlier earned a Bachelor's Degree in General Studies at age 95 and received recognition as a Guinness world record holder for oldest college graduate. Ochs shrugged off her accomplishments, "I'm not doing anything but what a lot of people have done, except I'm old." She's still in school, now working toward a Master of Arts in History.

Will I try for my masters? Perhaps when I'm a little older.

I once said in my early years (my 70s), "If senility wants me, it has to come in and drag me out, kicking and screaming." I don't tempt fate anymore, in senility or its sister term, dementia. Our bodies change on their natural course, and age is not always kind and gentle to us. Although we retain our vocabulary, IQ, and expertise, we wind down in the natural process of life as our body begins to wear out on its way to departure, clutching our one-way ticket. But according to the Longitudinal Study on Aging and the National Health Interview Survey, rates of disability are declining and recovery from acute disabilities improves steadily.

We all know the benefits and blessings of physical exercise, any kind that improves blood flow and enables heart, lungs and blood vessels to deliver oxygen to our muscles. Regular exercise can boost our heart rate and our memory. The good news is that walking is a low-impact activity and is one of the body's most natural and beneficial forms of exercise.

Do I exercise? Does it count when I walk through the house searching for my phone, cane, reading glasses or hearing aids? Walking briskly from one class to another and climbing steps on the campus is a superb memory. Now I feel my body snicker at some of my long-term plans that require physical activity. But I do exercise—moderately (at times getting out of bed in the morning is exercise). The reclining chair placed invitingly in front of the television often beckons, and though I sometimes accept its offerings, I am more apt to head for my computer and the magnetism it holds. But scouts honor—I do exercise my mind (maybe because it's less strenuous).

It's quite easy when our bodies start to falter, to place our minds in the same mode. Though it's impossible to predict memory loss, we can do our best to prevent it. Severe mental decline is usually caused by disease, whereas most age-related losses in memory are simply the result from inactivity, a lack of mental exercise and stimulation. As we keep physically active to keep our body more able to perform, we should exercise our mind to keep it sharp and agile.

Today, we learn the merits of the human brain and that anyone in reasonable health can improve its function. A complex and amazing piece of architecture, the brain continues to grow and is able to continually adapt and rewire itself. Even in old age, it can grow new neurons, new cells. An active brain also produces new dendrites, the connections between nerve cells that allow them to communicate with one another. But to create and nourish these new brain connections, we need to keep learning and challenging ourselves, to prod and push our minds to actively seek the new. The old cliché was right, use it or lose it.

To you who have "settled back" from the years of responsibility and productivity, suddenly, in a way, you are *you* again. It's a bit like coming home to yourself or starting a new chapter of your life. Now is the time to dust off the desires and goals of earlier years, and use your knowledge and experience in creative ways. You have the opportunity now to explore new ideas. Our best quality is our individual uniqueness and a firm belief in our potential at whatever our age. No, it's not always easy to reach out and grab onto new concepts, sometimes it's downright challenging, but it can be good to struggle along fresh and interesting roads, it increases our initiative and hones our skills. When we add something new and worthwhile to our lifestyle, something to challenge ourselves, it adds another dimension to our life.

Even self-directed learning can keep our minds active and opens up a whole new world for the trying. The media suggests we exercise our minds in gentle diversion by working crossword puzzles, and playing mind-stimulating word games. That's good advice, but our minds are much more capable than merely recalling information we know. Seek new experiences, socialize and become involved, read new books and magazines, follow current events, or enter the worthwhile cause of volunteering. The important thing is to experience new frontiers.

Engage in such simple pleasures as fly-fishing and woodworking, biking and bird watching, or choose exotic activities such as mountain climbing or hang-gliding. Belly dancing? Sure, there are lessons for that. But if your mobility is curtailed, as with many of us in later years, try your hand at quieter activities, drawing, sketching, painting, craft activities, needlework, or writing. Genealogy, tracing your family's roots, can be fascinating (finding a skeleton in your closet can give you a mental boost).

Each of us is a collection of unique experiences, so writing or recording our personal story, or the stories of others, can be rewarding. Most libraries, heritage centers and museums welcome the tapes made by older generations; many wonderful long-ago stories have been lost forever because no one listened or bothered to record them. Elders exclaim, "Oh, nobody would be interested in my early life, those things happened a long time ago." That's the point; it was a long time ago, in another era. Ask a question of them, and they may respond, "I don't remember," but wait patiently and they recall an item, and that leads to another item and another until you have their whole story.

We're all a component of history. Our deeds, however small, fit in a jigsaw fashion into the history of the era and the area in which we live. While some of us simply drift with the current of time, others ride the waves. These riders are doers with tales to tell, and while they live to tell them, we need to listen and preserve them. Names and dates and events tend to grow fuzzy with age and finally fade away, while documents and photographs go astray, unless we catch a point in time and record its history.

You like fiction? Many of us have a story rumbling around inside us. Who cares whether or not it sells—that's not the point—writing rattles our mind. You think you're not educated enough to write? Indeed you are. The short story course I took in college included the biography of each author; many of them had little or no formal education. I asked my professor how they could write with such limited learning. He answered, "You don't have to have an education to write."

Poetry? Write a poem—the first will lead to more. It doesn't have to rhyme, you know, but if you're really into rhyming, look for examples in books and online. Forget commercial greeting cards: compose funny, zany or serious poems tailored to the individuals—they will love them.

No time for writing? Baloney. You have the time to do about anything you really want to do. I wrote my first book with nine children at home. I took the story with me wherever I went and I wrote. Once I was hiding in bed with the light out, knees propped up, flashlight focused on my writing underneath the covers, all the time thinking, "this is ridiculous."

Can't write as well as others? Who can? As I struggled to form words, I whined that my writing was not as good as some letters to the editor I read. Then I came across a bit of wisdom by Henry Van Dyke: "Use the talent you possess. The world would be so silent if no birds sang except the best."

And more advice from the *Desiderata* by Max Ehrmann: "If you compare yourself with others you may become vain or bitter, for always there will be greater and lesser persons than yourself." I framed and hung these words above my desk, started writing—and stopped reading letters to the editor.

In the world of communication, technology expanded with the printing press, evolved into the telephone and spread widely with the Internet, allowing us to interact freely on a global scale. To place myself in perspective, I am indeed older than the first radio news program in 1920, and I was also fairly early for some of the first two-way tele-phones. Our first one, enclosed in a polished brown wooden case, a receiver on one side, hung on the wall, and as I stretched to talk, a courteous voice asked, "Number please." I've gone from that large sturdy model clear across the years to a small sleek know-it-all phone I slide in my pocket or stash in my purse. Did I program my phone? Well, no, my youngest grandchild did that, for I'm still working on how to remove the top from a childproof bottle.

But with zero mechanical ability, I've operated a computer for over twenty years. It and I are com-fortably close. It's the first I greet in the morning and the last I bid good night. Once, a visiting young grandson came to me and said, "Grand-mother, your computer is outdated." I answered, "mmmm..." Twenty minutes later he was back: "I don't know what happened, it just all disappeared." I followed him and looked at the black hole in dis-may. My life had vanished, my email messages, correspondence, photos, bank online, all my writ-ings including innards of a book I was composing, other manuscripts, historical presentations and col-lege essays, all gone. But the beauty in my life is that each member of my extended family is computer-savvy. A son from Houston flew in and recovered it all.

Some of you may say: "That's why I don't want one of those contraptions." But you might reconsider owning a computer. Once we master the basic skills of operation (at any age), those contraptions usually run smoothly, opening up a whole new world of wonder with email, websites and the Internet to keep our minds operating. Of course, it's far easier to maintain a computer if we have family members or friends to call on for help (and the younger they are, the more quickly they can help).

Other ways to keep our mind agile involves music, for its joy and beauty can uplift our spirits. When we experience the creativity of a musical piece, it can take us a step beyond the practical world. And many seniors find playing a musical instrument can keep the mind alert late in life. Roy Ernst, who taught 25 years at the Eastman School of Music in Rochester, New York, designed a program in 1991 for the 50-plus population. He explained:

If you once played an instrument, or want to learn, you can pick it up. It was once believed if you didn't learn music in childhood you missed your chance. High school kids could never do what we do, because they haven't lived enough, they haven't seen enough joy or sorrow. We have a special ability to play music expressively and with feeling.

So if you're interested in getting involved with instrumental music, look for a senior-band in your area. If there is no senior band available in your area see the website www.Newhorizonsmusic.org. If you are interested in learning a musical instrument on your own, find a teacher willing to take on an older student.

And yes, travel if you can. Many of us mortals view our world as within a few miles of our home territory, a domain that's secure and familiar, and we have little curiosity as to what's out there. In reality a world of enchantment beyond comprehension is out there. If you have the resources and want to shake your perspective, take a trip, perhaps where you've never been and as far as your funds will stretch. You'll find travel can almost wipe out stress. As you know, however, it's harder now for you and your baggage to leave the airport, but once airborne you're relatively safe. I hear others say, "I wouldn't want to go to Europe or any such place; I haven't seen all the states in my own country." Well, then, see those states if you can. Gather a bundle of learning and start a lifetime treasury of memories.

When we landed in Paris, my first impression was instant fascination and romance (go to Paris with someone you love). Everything is *so old and so cherished,* as were structures in other European countries. We are so hurried here, things are so new, almost as if the wrappings aren't off...how long will it take to put up that house, that building, the church, what will it cost?

But you say, you're not ready for another project, a new adventure; you've completed your self-imposed path and you've earned a rest. Indeed you have, it's understandable. Rest is important, but when we choose leisure and become content in our comfortable chairs, we may be choosing to be less than we could be. It's easy to slip into the inevitable signs of aging with its inflexibility of opinions and habits and its resistance to change. Are we watching the lives of others play out, living our lives vicariously? We hear that life is a card game; we play the hand we're dealt. True, it's your card game; but maybe you should shuffle the cards and slip in a wild one.

Many of you who retired are trained and experienced and may need or desire to supplement your income in some way. Despite stereotypes that older workers may be slower, studies show they are often more productive and have a higher level of loyalty and commitment. You can research job possibilities, some with help from a local professional agency and others from the Internet. Money may be made at home with patience and imagination. Search for "15 crazy ways people make money" on the Internet for an eye-opener.

So choose your pursuit or goal, be it ever so small. Don't put your mind on hold, put it on roam and plant your first step on a chosen path in a new direction. Whatever your age, you're never too old for your next project, your next career.

And really, for many of us, aging isn't all that devastating, is it? Life isn't all we want, but it's all we've got, so we may as well stick a daisy in our hat and rest content.

And keep an eye out for butterflies and rainbows along the way. I visited my six great-granddaughters recently, and as we walked to a nearby park they mentioned they sometimes see snakes. Immediately I began watching where I walked. One of the small girls said, "Don't look for snakes, Grandmother, look for butterflies."

I read a great deal, especially the newspaper notices of wedding anniversaries, the 50, 60 and even 70 years of togetherness. I wonder what their lives are like (they smile in the photos). I wonder if they have grown closer together in their interests, or since marriage is a matter of give and take, did one interest supersede or include the other?

I also read obituaries. I find many people have lived rich active lives with work, travel, volunteering, and hobbies. I chanced across an obituary of Anna Amelia Furlow, a lovely lady from Lamesa, Texas, who died November 26, 2005 at the age of 84.

According to the article, "Amelia held tightly to her principles of being a good Christian, loving and faithful wife and protector of her family." The quality of "protector" extended to "bravely accompanying her husband Lance several times a week on his favorite hobby of rattlesnake hunting, brandishing a hoe until he made the kill with slingshot."

Lance, at 95, still lives at home, and according to his daughter Carmen, relates snake stories and proudly displays his trophies of the many rattler tails he took from his prey.   He tries to get his children to take him snake hunting.   But they, not imbued with the hardy spirit of the plains' settlers of West Texas who could wrestle their predator to the ground, say they want something more powerful than a hoe.

So, is Lance old?   Who defines age?   At what age are we old?   Samuel Ullman who started writing in his late years, defined youth and oldness:

Youth is not a time of life; it is a state of mind...it is a matter of will, a quality of the imagination, a vigor of the emotions; it is a freshness of the deep springs of life. Nobody grows old merely by living a number of years... we grow old by deserting our ideals...whether sixty or sixteen, there is in every human being's heart the lure of wonder, the unfailing child-like curiosity of what's next, and the joy of the game of living. In the center of your heart and mind there is a wireless station; so long as it receives messages of beauty, hope, cheer and courage, you are young.

When the aerials are down, and your spirit is covered with the snows of cynicism and the ice of pessimism, then you have grown old, even at twenty.

Indeed You Can

On a personal note: I began this long conversation with you on a note of learning; and I'll end it as that.

If you develop a passion for learning, you'll never be bored. The opportunity for increasing our knowledge is all around us, for we live in a world that hangs ripe with fascinating facts. All we have to do is reach up and pluck them off the ample trees of knowledge, if only we are curious and motivated to keep learning.

Curiosity packs a wallop into the game of learning; it provides food for the brain, giving it mental exercise that strengthens it over time. But aside from that, it enriches our lives; curious people are always looking for answers to questions they encounter; they thrive on knowledge, turning learning into a lifelong process that keeps their mind active. Curious people are always working on a project, stretching to reach a goal, seeking to find answers to their innumerable questions, immersed in the tantalizing world of wonder. New worlds and possibilities lie within their grasp to be discovered by a curious mind.

Curiosity is an innate basic emotion that can be developed. Keep an open mind; watch for new ideas and information. Reach below the surface of what you see and experience in life; ask questions incessantly...who, what, when, where, why and how. Curiosity is a trait of the genius (you do want to be a genius, don't you?)

In my years of searching for answers in writing history, I learned to research deeply into a topic. A history professor at Sul Ross University at Alpine, Texas, told me, "I've written and taught history for a multitude of years, but I've never seen a writer that can research like you. You don't accept answers that are apparent, you keep digging until you unearth the small fascinating facts that make the difference."

I'm glad I'm an opsimath with an affinity for words. I'd not trade that for a barrel of gold nuggets.

Someone said that growth in old age requires the curiosity of a five-year-old and the confidence of a teenager. It also requires the by-golly attitude of "indeed I can."

9 781926 918532